Pearls
of
Wisdom

Pearls
of
Wisdom

Harvested by

JEROME AGEL

and

WALTER D. GLANZE

Quill
A HarperResource Book
An Imprint of HarperCollins*Publishers*

Harper & Row, Publishers, New York
Cambridge, Philadelphia, San Francisco, Washington
London, Mexico City, São Paulo, Singapore, Sydney

FIRST EDITION

Designed by Lydia Link

Library of Congress Cataloging-in-Publication Data

Agel, Jerome.
  Pearls of wisdom.

  Includes index.
  1. Quotations, English.   I. Glanze, Walter D.
II. Title.
PN6081.A44   1987   082   87-45016
ISBN 0-06-096200-3 (pbk.)

05   RRD-H 30 29

Preface

He is a benefactor of mankind who contracts the great
rules of life into short sentences, that may be easily
impressed on the memory, and so recur habitually to
the mind.

Samuel Johnson

We couldn't have said it better ourselves!

Jerome Agel and Walter D. Glanze

The best way to make your dreams come true is to
wake up.
Paul Valéry

Let us endeavor so to live that when we come to die
even the undertaker will be sorry.
Mark Twain

To speak of "mere words" is much like speaking of
"mere dynamite."
C. J. Ducasse

A man's real worth is determined by what he does
when he has nothing to do.
Megiddo Message

The excellent is new forever.
Ralph Waldo Emerson

[1]

There is no distance on this earth as far away as yesterday.

Robert Nathan

That old law about "an eye for an eye" leaves everybody blind.

Martin Luther King, Jr.

If the only tool you have is a hammer, you tend to see every problem as a nail.

Abraham Maslow

Wise people, even though all laws were abolished, would still lead the same life.

Aristophanes (ca. 200 B.C.)

Time is the music of our being. It is to us what water is to fish.

Jessica Julian

[2]

You can't hold a man down without staying down
with him.

Booker T. Washington

The wise don't expect to find life worth living; they
make it that way.

Anonymous

Nothing is so firmly believed as what is least
known.

*Michel Eyquem de Montaigne
(16th century)*

Real generosity is doing something nice for someone
who'll never find it out.

Frank A. Clark

Whenever I draw a circle, I immediately want to
step out of it.

R. Buckminster Fuller

There is no pillow so soft as a clear conscience.

European saying

Absence diminishes weak passions and increases great ones, as the wind blows out candles and fans fire.

François de La Rochefoucauld
(17th century)

Great is the human who has not lost his childlike heart.

Mencius (Meng-Tse)
(4th century B.C.)

Each day should be passed as though it were our last.

Publilius Syrus (ca. 50 B.C.)

The reasonable man adapts himself to the world; the unreasonable one persists in trying to adapt the world to himself. Therefore all progress depends on the unreasonable man.

George Bernard Shaw

Silence. All human unhappiness comes from not knowing how to stay quietly in a room.

Blaise Pascal (17th century)

Whatever else there may be in our nature, responsibility toward truth is one of its attributes.

Arthur Eddington

A friend is a present you give yourself.

Robert Louis Stevenson

Once the game is over, the king and the pawn go back into the same box.
Italian saying

Doubt everything at least once, even the sentence "Two times two is four."
Georg Christoph Lichtenberg

You cannot be both fashionable and first-rate.
Logan Pearsall Smith

It is humans that make truth great, not truth that makes humans great.
Confucius (ca. 500 B.C.)

If you want something done, ask a busy person.
Benjamin Franklin

There's always room for improvement—it's the biggest room in the house.
Louise Heath Leber

Believe that life is worth living, and your belief will help create the fact.
William James

Not knowing when the dawn will come
I open every door.
Emily Dickinson

The feeble tremble before opinion, the foolish defy it, the wise judge it, the skillful direct it.
Jeanne Roland

Only those who will risk going too far can possibly find out how far one can go.
T. S. Eliot

[7]

Treat people as if they were what they should be, and you help them become what they are capable of becoming.

Johann Wolfgang von Goethe

Resolved, never to do anything which I should be afraid to do if it were the last hour of my life.

Jonathan Edwards

People will believe anything if you whisper it.

Anonymous

It is only those who never do anything who never make mistakes.

A. Favre

Everyone is ignorant, only on different subjects.

Will Rogers

Every man has a right to be wrong in his opinions. But no man has a right to be wrong about his facts.

Bernard Baruch

No one can make you feel inferior without your consent.

Eleanor Roosevelt

It is not the answer that enlightens, but the question.

Eugène Ionesco

Always let losers have their words.

Francis Bacon (ca. 1600)

A man's real possession is his memory. In nothing else is he rich, in nothing else is he poor.

Alexander Smith

[9]

Behold the turtle. He makes progress only when he sticks his neck out.

James B. Conant

Show them the death, and they will accept the fever.

Arab saying

We all live under the same sky, but we don't all have the same horizon.

Konrad Adenauer

Life can only be understood backwards; but it must be lived forwards.

Sören Kierkegaard

A genius is one who shoots at something no one else can see, and hits it.

Anonymous

See everything; overlook a great deal; correct a little.
Pope John XXIII

The Wright brothers flew right through the smoke
screen of impossibility.
Charles Franklin Kettering

The belief that youth is the happiest time of life is
founded on a fallacy. The happiest person is
the person who thinks the most interesting
thoughts, and we grow happier as we grow
older.
William Lyon Phelps

What a man really has, is what is in him. What is
outside of him, should be a matter of no
importance.
Oscar Wilde

Imagination is more important than knowledge.

Albert Einstein

I have learned to use the word *impossible* with the greatest caution.

Wernher von Braun

To be able to dispense with good things is tantamount to possessing them.

Jean François Regnard (17th century)

Young. Old. Just words.

George Burns (at age 84)

The most exquisite pleasure is giving pleasure to others.

Jean de La Bruyère (17th century)

The first and great commandment is, Don't let them scare you.

Elmer Davis

There are children playing in the street who could solve some of my top problems in physics, because they have modes of sensory perception that I lost long ago.

J. Robert Oppenheimer

The important thing in life is not the triumph but the struggle.

Pierre de Coubertin

I don't like work—no man does—but I like what is in work—the chance to find yourself.

Joseph Conrad

Culture is the habit of being pleased with the best and knowing why.
>> Henry Van Dyke

Every perfect traveler always creates the country where he travels.
>> Nikos Kazantzakis

How many people are killed in accidents because of not wanting to let go of their umbrellas!
>> Paul Valéry

Making the simple complicated is commonplace; making the complicated simple, awesomely simple, that's creativity.
>> Charles Mingus

Dying is easy, comedy is hard.
>> Edmund Gwenn

If in the last few years you haven't discarded a major
opinion or acquired a new one, check your
pulse. You may be dead.
Gelett Burgess

Do not free a camel of the burden of his hump; you
may be freeing him from being a camel.
G. K. Chesterton

Life shrinks or expands in proportion to one's
courage.
Anaïs Nin

We can easily forgive a child who is afraid of the
dark; the real tragedy of life is when adults are
afraid of the light.
Plato (ca. 400 B.C.)

Experience is a hard teacher. She gives the test first, the lesson afterwards.

Anonymous

I find the great thing in this world is not so much where we stand, as in what direction we are moving.

Oliver Wendell Holmes, Jr.

Defer not till tomorrow to be wise,
Tomorrow's sun to thee may never rise.

William Congreve

There is no exercise better for the heart than reaching down and lifting people up.

John Andrew Holmer

The greatest right in the world is the right to be wrong.

Harry Weinberger

The truly civilized man is always skeptical and
        tolerant. . . . His culture is based on "I am not
        too sure."
                    H. L. Mencken

To burn always with a hard, gemlike flame, that's
        success in life.
                    Robert W. Marks

Wit consists in knowing the resemblance of things
        that differ, and the difference of things that
        are alike.
                    Madame de Staël

Nothing will ever be attempted if all possible
        objections must be first overcome.
                    Samuel Johnson

Trouble is a sieve through which we sift our
  acquaintances. Those too big to pass through
  are our friends.
                                        Arlene Francis

Getting an idea should be like sitting down on a
  pin; it should make you jump up and do
  something.
                                        E. L. Simpson

The proof that the human being is the noblest of all
  creatures is that no other creature has ever
  denied it.
                                Georg Christoph Lichtenberg

To get nowhere, follow the crowd.
                                        Anonymous

If you judge people, you have no time to love them.
                                        Mother Teresa

Maturity of mind is the capacity to endure
   uncertainty.

John Finley

Is it ever happiness that we seek? No, it is the free
   play of those forces that happen to be the most
   recent ones in us.

André Gide (at age 80)

On the human chessboard, all moves are possible.

Miriam Schiff

The main thing is that you hear life's music
   everywhere. Most people hear only its
   dissonances.

Theodor Fontane

A person has two legs and one sense of humor, and if you're faced with the choice, it's better to lose a leg.

Charles Lindner

Even the highest towers begin from the ground.

Chinese saying

People who drink to drown their sorrow should be told that sorrow knows how to swim.

Ann Landers

Love is staying up all night with a sick child—or a healthy adult.

David Frost

Memory is the only paradise from which no one can drive us.

Jean Paul (Friedrich Richter)

The hottest places in hell are reserved for those who, in a period of moral crisis, maintain their neutrality.

Dante Alighieri (ca. 1300)

There is no season such delight can bring,
as summer, autumn, winter, and the spring.

William Browne

If something is boring after two minutes, try it for four. If still boring, try it for eight, sixteen, thirty-two, and so on. Eventually, one discovers that it is not boring but very interesting.

Zen saying

Be ashamed to die until you have won one victory for humanity.

Horace Mann

They say they climb mountains because they are
  there. I wonder if it would astound them to
  know that the very same reason is why the rest
  of us go around them.

S. Omar Barker

When it is dark enough, you can see the stars.

Charles Beard

Losing an illusion makes you wiser than finding
  a truth.

Ludwig Börne

Whatever you cannot understand, you cannot
  possess.

Johann Wolfgang von Goethe

If men believe, as I do, that this present earth is the only heaven, they will strive all the more to make heaven of it.

Sir Arthur Keith

You will find rest from vanities if you go about every act in life as though it were your last.

Marcus Aurelius (2nd century A.D.)

We cannot first think and act afterwards. From the moment of birth we are immersed in action, and can only fitfully guide it by taking thought.

Alfred North Whitehead

What is noble can be said in any language, and what is mean should be said in none.

Maimonides (12th century)

Forgiveness is the finding again of a lost possession—
hatred an extended suicide.

Friedrich Schiller

Life is just a series of trying to make up your mind.

Timothy Fuller

The eyes of other people are the eyes that ruin us.
If all but myself were blind, I should want
neither fine clothes, fine houses, nor fine
furniture.

Benjamin Franklin

Happiness is a by-product of an effort to make
someone else happy.

Gretta Brooker Palmer

The time to win a fight is before it starts.

Frederick W. Lewis

Where love is concerned, too much is not even
enough.

Pierre-Augustin Caron
de Beaumarchais

Nobody will ever win the battle of the sexes.
There's too much fraternizing with the enemy.

Henry Kissinger

It ain't so much what people don't know that hurts as
what they know that ain't so.

Artemus Ward

Death accompanies us at every step and enables us
to use those moments when life smiles at us to
feel more deeply the sweetness of life. The
more certain the end, the more tempting the
minute.

Theodor Fontane

The mightiest lever known to the moral world,
Imagination.
William Wordsworth

He only profits from praise who values criticism.
Heinrich Heine

If you wish to make an apple pie truly from scratch,
you must first invent the universe.
Carl Sagan

The spirit of liberty is the spirit that's not too sure it's
right.
Learned Hand

The real purpose of books is to trap the mind into
doing its own thinking.
Christopher Morley

[26]

I have the greatest of all riches: that of not desiring
   them.

Eleonora Duse

We are here to add what we can to life, not to get
   what we can from it.

William Osler

Unrest of spirit is a mark of life.

Karl Menninger

True wit is nature to advantage dressed,
      What oft was thought, but ne'er so well
   expressed.

Alexander Pope

It is better to wear out than to rust out.

Richard Cumberland (17th century)

[27]

A foolish consistency is the hobgoblin of little minds.

Ralph Waldo Emerson

Tact consists in knowing how far to go too far.

Jean Cocteau

People want peace so badly that governments ought to get out of their way and let them have it.

Dwight D. Eisenhower

Truth is fire, and to speak the truth means to illuminate and burn.

L. Schefer

To a large degree reality is whatever the people who are around at the time agree to.

Milton H. Miller

Wit ought to be a glorious treat, like caviar; never spread it about like marmalade.

Noël Coward

Genius is an infinite capacity for taking pains.

Jane Ellice Hopkins

To think is easy. To act is difficult. To act as one thinks is the most difficult of all.

Johann Wolfgang von Goethe

People who are sensible about love are incapable of it.

Douglas Yates

The world is moving so fast these days that the man who says it can't be done is generally interrupted by someone doing it.

Elbert Hubbard

A room without books is like a body without a soul.

Marcus Tullius Cicero
(1st century B.C.)

Every man in the world is better than someone else.
And not as good as someone else.

William Saroyan

Character is simply habit long enough continued.

Plutarch (ca. A.D. 100)

Loyalty to petrified opinion never yet broke a chain
or freed a human soul.

Mark Twain

A beautiful woman who gives pleasure to men
serves only to frighten the fish when she jumps
in the water.

Kwang-Tse

[30]

Time is the most valuable thing one can spend.

Theophrastus (ca. 300 B.C.)

Live as you will wish to have lived when you are
dying.

Christian Fürchtegott Gellert

Don't wait for George to do it, because he won't.

Jessica Julian

It is well that there is no one without a fault; for he
would not have a friend in the world. He
would seem to belong to a different species.

William Hazlitt

You should be more afraid of a stupid man than of an
evil one.

Christina of Sweden (17th century)

Wisdom ofttimes consists of knowing what to do next.

Herbert Hoover

A diamond is a chunk of coal that made good under pressure.

Anonymous

Tact is the great ability to see other people as they think you see them.

Carl Zuckmayer

The educated person is someone who knows how to find out what he doesn't know.

Georg Simmel

The simplest and shortest ethical precept is to be served by others as little as possible, and to serve others as much as possible.

Leo Tolstoy

[32]

The man who trusts other men will make fewer
mistakes than he who distrusts them.
Camillo di Cavour

The sun, with all those planets revolving around it
and dependent on it, can still ripen a bunch of
grapes as if it had nothing else in the universe
to do.
Galileo Galilei (ca. 1600)

Any place I hang my hat is home.
Johnny Mercer

No one is exempt from talking nonsense; the
misfortune is to do it solemnly.
*Michel Eyquem de Montaigne
(16th century)*

To do great and important tasks, two things are
necessary: a plan and not quite enough time.
Anonymous

[33]

Everything comes to him who hustles while he
waits.

Thomas Alva Edison

The mark of the immature man is that he wants to
die nobly for a cause, while the mark of the
mature man is that he wants to live humbly for
one.

Wilhelm Stekel

Words can bruise and break hearts, and minds as
well. There are no black and blue marks, no
broken bones to put in plaster cast, and
therefore no prison bars for the offender.

Marlene Dietrich

History doesn't pass the dishes again.

Louis-Ferdinand Céline

It is the greatest of advantages to enjoy no advantage at all.

Henry David Thoreau

One of the advantages of being disorderly is that one is constantly making exciting discoveries.

A. A. Milne

Please all, and you will please none.

Aesop (ca. 550 B.C.)

Philosophy is nothing but discretion.

John Selden (17th century)

To wish to progress is the largest part of progress.

Lucius Annaeus Seneca
(1st century A.D.)

Seek simplicity, and distrust it.
> *Alfred North Whitehead*

If the temper of your mind gets interwoven with your convictions, you lose in heat what you might gain by reason.
> *Margot Asquith*

Life is like playing a violin solo in public and learning the instrument as one goes on.
> *Samuel Butler (19th century)*

I have a simple philosophy. Fill what's empty. Empty what's full. And scratch where it itches.
> *Alice Roosevelt Longworth*

Give a man a fish, and you feed him for a day; teach him to fish—and you feed him for a lifetime.
> *Native American saying*

Be glad of life because it gives you the chance to
    love and to work and to play and to look up at
    the stars.

Henry Van Dyke

I am not afraid of tomorrow, for I have seen
    yesterday and I love today.

William Allen White

The person who pursues revenge should dig two
    graves.

Old proverb

It has ever been my experience that folks who have no
    vices have very few virtues.

Abraham Lincoln

A word once let out of the cage cannot be whistled
    back again.

Horace (1st century B.C.)

[37]

We are what we pretend to be, so we must be careful about what we pretend to be.

Kurt Vonnegut

If you treat a sick child like an adult and a sick adult like a child, everything usually works out pretty well.

Ruth Carlisle

A problem adequately stated is a problem well on its way to being solved.

R. Buckminster Fuller

To live is to be slowly born.

Antoine de Saint-Exupéry

Human beings love company even if it is only that of a small burning candle.

Georg Christoph Lichtenberg

[38]

The mere sense of living is joy enough.
                    Emily Dickinson

If what you are telling is true, you don't have to
    choose your words so carefully.
                    Frank A. Clark

Wait for that wisest of all counselors, Time.
                    Pericles (ca. 450 B.C.)

A proverb distills the wisdom of the ages, and only a
    fool is scornful of the commonplace.
                    William Somerset Maugham

Think of the totality of all Being, and what a mite of
    it is yours; think of all Time, and the brief
    fleeting instant of it that is allotted to yourself;
    think of Destiny, and how puny a part of it
    you are.
                    Marcus Aurelius (2nd century A.D.)

No mind is thoroughly well organized that is
deficient in a sense of humor.

Samuel Taylor Coleridge

You're never too old to become younger.

Mae West

The measure of success is not whether you have a
tough problem to deal with, but whether it's
the same problem you had last year.

John Foster Dulles

I always prefer to believe the best of everybody—it
saves so much trouble.

Rudyard Kipling

Making music is another way of making children.

Friedrich Nietzsche

Good humor is one of the best articles of dress one can wear in society.

William Makepeace Thackeray

If we begin with certainties, we shall end in doubts; but if we begin with doubts, and are patient, we shall end in certainties.

Francis Bacon (ca. 1600)

The one who lives the longest and the one who lives the shortest, when it comes to dying lose one and the same thing.

Marcus Aurelius (2nd century A.D.)

The highest purpose is to have no purpose at all. This puts one in accord with nature, in her manner of operation.

John Cage

If you are not part of the solution, you are part of the problem.

Eldridge Cleaver

We all know it isn't human to be perfect, and too many of us take advantage of it.

Anonymous

Believe nothing, no matter where you read it, or who said it, no matter if I have said it, unless it agrees with your own reason and your own common sense.

Buddha (6th century B.C.)

It doesn't hurt to be optimistic. You can always cry later.

Lucimar Santos de Lima

Even if you're on the right track, you'll get run over if you just sit there.

Will Rogers

Live all you can; it's a mistake not to. It doesn't so much matter what you do in particular, so long as you have had your life. If you haven't had that, what have you had?

Henry James

He's an honest man—you could shoot craps with him over the telephone.

Earl Wilson

Give a man health and a course to steer, and he'll never stop to trouble about whether he's happy or not.

George Bernard Shaw

[43]

A fallacy that makes me glad
Is worth a truth that makes me sad.
Christoph Martin Wieland

To teach is to learn twice.
Joseph Joubert

We live amid surfaces, and the true art is to skate
well on them.
Ralph Waldo Emerson

Nothing endures but change.
Heraclitus (ca. 500 B.C.)

The soul is born old but grows young. That is the
comedy of life. And the body is born young
and grows old. That is life's tragedy.
Oscar Wilde

[44]

You can tell more about a person by what he says
about others than you can by what others say
about him.

Leo Aikman

I'm not happy, I'm cheerful. There's a difference. A
happy woman has no cares at all. A cheerful
woman has cares but has learned how to deal
with them.

Beverly Sills

You can never have a greater or a lesser dominion
than that over yourself.

Leonardo da Vinci (ca. 1500)

Circumstances are the rulers of the weak; they are
but the instruments of the wise.

Samuel Lover

They [the good old days] were never that good, believe me. The good new days are today, and better days are coming tomorrow. Our greatest songs are still unsung.

Hubert H. Humphrey

Besides the noble art of getting things done, there is the noble art of leaving things undone. The wisdom of life consists in the elimination of nonessentials.

Lin Yutang

If one is lucky, a solitary fantasy can totally transform one million realities.

Maya Angelou

We are more often frightened than hurt; and we suffer more from imagination than from reality.

*Lucius Annaeus Seneca
(1st century A.D.)*

There never was a good war or a bad peace.

Benjamin Franklin

Your sole contribution to the sum of things is
yourself.

Frank Crane

What is soul? It's like electricity—we don't really
know what it is, but it's a force that can light a
room.

Ray Charles

All books will become light in proportion as you
find light in them.

Mortimer J. Adler

A person who doesn't know but knows that he doesn't know is a student; teach him. A person who knows but who doesn't know that he knows is asleep; awaken him. But a person who knows and knows that he knows is wise; follow him.

Old Asian proverb

Freedom is not worth having if it does not include the freedom to make mistakes.

Mahatma Gandhi

Many a time I have wanted to stop talking and find out what I really believed.

Walter Lippmann

Whatever is worth doing at all, is worth doing well.

Earl of Chesterfield

Whenever one finds oneself inclined to bitterness, it is a sign of emotional failure.

Bertrand Russell

I am erecting a barrier of simplicity between myself and the world.

André Gide

I believe fervently in our species and have no patience with the current fashion of running down the human being. On the contrary, we are a spectacular, splendid manifestation of life. We matter. We are the newest, youngest, brightest thing around.

Lewis Thomas

We should be taught not to wait for inspiration to start a thing. Action always generates inspiration. Inspiration seldom generates action.

Frank Tibolt

We should stop kidding ourselves. We should let go of things that aren't true. It's always better with the truth.

R. Buckminster Fuller

Immunity to boredom gives the computer the edge.

Alan Lakein

If one is too lazy to think, too vain to do a thing badly, too cowardly to admit it, one will never attain wisdom.

Cyril Connolly

Words, like eyeglasses, blur everything that they do not make more clear.

Joseph Joubert

Courage is resistance to fear, mastery of fear, not absence of fear.

Mark Twain

You cease to be afraid when you cease to hope; for hope is accompanied by fear.

Lucius Annaeus Seneca
(1st century A.D.)

Solitude is fine, but you need someone to tell you that solitude is fine.

Honoré de Balzac

Few are they who have never had the chance to achieve happiness—and fewer those who have taken that chance.

André Maurois

As a matter of fact, no man can be merry unless he is serious. Happiness is as grave and practical as sorrow, if not more so.

G. K. Chesterton

Don't be angry that you cannot make others as you wish them to be, because you cannot make yourself as you wish to be.

Thomas à Kempis (15th century)

Less is more—more or less.

Ludwig Miës van der Rohe

You're not as young as you used to be, but you're not as old as you're going to be. So watch it!

Irish proverb

We think in generalities, we live in detail.

Alfred North Whitehead

To select well among old things is almost equal to inventing new ones.

Nicolas Charles Trublet

[52]

In this world there are only two tragedies. One is not getting what one wants, and the other is getting it.

Oscar Wilde

The limits of my language mean the limits of my world.

Ludwig Wittgenstein

Every survival kit should include a sense of humor.

Anonymous

Common sense is genius dressed in its working clothes.

Ralph Waldo Emerson

Nothing worse could happen to one than to be completely understood.

Carl Gustav Jung

Love consists in this: that two solitudes protect and touch and greet each other.

Rainer Maria Rilke

Silence is a true friend who never betrays.

Confucius (ca. 500 B.C.)

If blood be shed, let it be our blood. Cultivate the quiet courage of dying without killing. For man lives freely only by his readiness to die, if need be, at the hands of his brother, never by killing him.

Mahatma Gandhi

We forfeit three-fourths of ourselves in order to be like other people.

Arthur Schopenhauer

The thing of it is, we must live with the living.

Michel Eyquem de Montaigne
(16th century)

The road uphill and the road downhill are one and
the same.

Heraclitus (ca. 500 B.C.)

Memory is a net: one finds it full of fish when he
takes it from the brook, but a dozen miles of
water have run through it without sticking.

Oliver Wendell Holmes, Sr.

We are shaped and fashioned by what we love.

Johann Wolfgang von Goethe

Get your mind accustomed to doubting and your
heart to being conciliatory.

Georg Christoph Lichtenberg

Simplicity is the most difficult thing to secure in this
world; it is the last limit of experience and the
last effort of genius.

George Sand

[55]

The most wasted of all our days are those in which we have not laughed.

Nicolas-Sebastien de Chamfort

I envy the animals two things—their ignorance of evil to come, and their ignorance of what is said about them.

Voltaire

It's better to recall something you wish you'd said than something you wish you hadn't.

Frank A. Clark

We have two ears, but only one mouth, so that we may listen more and talk less.

Zeno (3rd century B.C.)

Lost time was like a run in a stocking. It always got worse.

Anne Morrow Lindbergh

Most folks are about as happy as they make up
their minds to be.
Abraham Lincoln

No pleasure lasts if it's unseasoned by variety.
Publilius Syrus (ca. 50 B.C.)

Above all, do not lose your desire to walk.
Sören Kierkegaard

A little learning is a dangerous thing.
Alexander Pope

Dare to be naive.
R. Buckminster Fuller

Hot heads and cold hearts never solved anything.
Anonymous

Nothing is worth more than this day.

Johann Wolfgang von Goethe

In the practical use of our intellect, forgetting is as
important as remembering.

William James

There is no disguise that can for long conceal love
where it exists or simulate it where it does not.

*François de La Rochefoucauld
(17th century)*

The real voyage of discovery consists not in seeking
new landscapes, but in having new eyes.

Marcel Proust

The human being is the weakest reed in the world,
but it is a reed that thinks.

Blaise Pascal (17th century)

The shrewd guess, the fertile hypothesis, the
  courageous leap to a tentative conclusion—
  these are the most valuable coin of the thinker
  at work. But in most schools guessing is
  heavily penalized and is associated somehow
  with laziness.

Jerome S. Bruner

You must learn to drink the cup of life as it comes
  . . . without stirring it up from the bottom.
  That's where the bitter dregs are.

Agnes Turnbull

I never found the companion that was so
  companionable as solitude.

Joseph Addison

The way to love anything is to realize that it may
  be lost.

G. K. Chesterton

It is happier to be sometimes cheated than not to
trust.

Samuel Johnson

Love is never lost. If not reciprocated, it will flow
back and soften and purify the heart.

Washington Irving

Nothing lays itself open to the charge of
exaggeration more than the language of naked
truth.

Joseph Conrad

The art of being wise is the art of knowing what to
overlook.

William James

Anybody who knows everything should be told a
thing or two.

Franklin P. Jones

I'd like to live like a poor man—only with lots of money.

Pablo Picasso

Many live in the ivory tower called reality; they never venture on the open sea of thought.

François Gautier

One of the secrets of a long and fruitful life is to forgive everybody everything every night before you go to bed.

Anonymous (quoted by Ann Landers)

Experience is not what happens to you; it is what you do with what happens to you.

Aldous Huxley

Everything should be made as simple as possible, but not simpler.

Albert Einstein

From each according to his abilities, to each
according to his needs.

Karl Marx

In this world, you must be a bit too kind to be kind
enough.

Pierre Carlet de Chamblain
de Marivaux

Nobody can contribute to the best of humanity who
does not make the best out of himself.

Johann Gottfried Herder

Life consists not in holding good cards, but in
playing well those you do hold.

Josh Billings

The classroom—not the trench—is the frontier of
freedom now and forevermore.

Lyndon Baines Johnson

O ne can live well even in a palace.

Marcus Aurelius (2nd century A.D.)

I f you want to be thought a liar, always tell the truth.

Logan Pearsall Smith

W ear your learning like your watch, in a private pocket; and do not pull it out and strike it merely to show that you have one. If you are asked what o'clock it is, tell it; but do not proclaim it hourly and unasked, like the watchman.

Earl of Chesterfield

T hey are never alone that are accompanied by noble thoughts.

Philip Sydney (16th century)

Never be haughty to the humble. Never be humble to the haughty.

Jefferson Davis

Don't part with your illusions. When they are gone, you may still exist, but you have ceased to live.

Mark Twain

If a man be gracious and courteous to strangers, it shows he is a citizen of the world, and that his heart is no island cut off from other lands, but a continent that joins to them.

Francis Bacon (ca. 1600)

Property given away is the only kind that will forever be yours.

Martial (1st century A.D.)

Illusions commend themselves to us because they save us pain and allow us to enjoy pleasure instead. We must therefore accept it without complaint when they sometimes collide with a bit of reality against which they are dashed to pieces.

Sigmund Freud

Everyone prefers belief to the exercise of judgment.

Lucius Annaeus Seneca
(1st century A.D.)

Men take more pains to mask than mend.

Benjamin Franklin

Circles though small are yet complete.

Anonymous

Doubt is not a very pleasant status, but certainty is a ridiculous one.

Voltaire

W̲hat a mistake to believe that by letting oneself go
naturally, one is, or becomes, the most
personal! Only commonplaces and clichés come
to one naturally and right off. Vulgarity
absorbs him who "lets himself go." The heavy
law of gravity holds us all.

André Gide

C̲ommon sense is instinct. Enough of it is genius.

George Bernard Shaw

I̲f a man finds himself with bread in both hands, he
should exchange one loaf for some flowers of
the narcissus, because the loaf feeds the body,
but the flowers feed the soul.

Muhammad (ca. 600 A.D.)

Make it a point to do something every day that you don't want to do. This is the golden rule for acquiring the habit of doing your duty without pain.

Mark Twain

Nothing in life is to be feared. It is only to be understood.

Marie Curie

Facing it—always facing it—that's the way to get through. Face it!

Joseph Conrad

We would have much peace if we would not busy ourselves with the sayings and doings of others.

Thomas à Kempis (15th century)

The best cure for hypochondria is to forget about your body and get interested in someone else's.

Goodman Ace

Thinking is more interesting than knowing, but not than looking.

Johann Wolfgang von Goethe

Truth is not a crystal that you can stash away in your pocket, it is an infinite liquid into which you fall.

Robert von Musil

The man who insists upon seeing with perfect clearness before he decides, never decides.

Henri Frédéric Amiel

Dying is no accomplishment; we all do that. Living is the thing.

Red Smith

Happiness belongs to those who are sufficient unto
themselves. For all external sources of
happiness and pleasure are, by their very
nature, highly uncertain, precarious,
ephemeral, and subject to chance.

Arthur Schopenhauer

No one knows what he is able to do until he tries.

Publilius Syrus (ca. 50 B.C.)

Self-reverence, self-knowledge, self-control
These three alone lead life to sovereign power.

Alfred Tennyson

The best throw of the dice is to throw them away.

Austin O'Malley

Vice is waste of life.

George Bernard Shaw

Growing old is no more than a bad habit that a busy person has no time to form.

André Maurois

We make a living by what we get, but we make a life by what we give.

Norman MacEwan

First health, then wealth, then pleasure, and do not owe anything to anybody.

Catherine the Great

Great Spirit, grant that I may not criticize my neighbor until I have walked a mile in his moccasins.

Native American saying

There is no education like adversity.

Benjamin Disraeli

No one is as poor as he who is ignorant.
Nedarim

Speech is civilization itself. The word, even the most contradictory word, preserves contact—it is silence that isolates.
Thomas Mann

The heart has reasons that reason does not know.
Blaise Pascal (17th century)

A long life may not be good enough, but a good life is long enough.
Quoted by Benjamin Franklin

Pleasure is very seldom found where it is sought.
Samuel Johnson

Time is nature's way of keeping everything from
      happening at once.

                 Anonymous

Neither the sun nor death can be looked fully in the
      face.

            François de La Rochefoucauld
            (17th century)

We find comfort among those who agree with us—
      growth among those who don't.

            Frank A. Clark

After a little of Einstein there ought to be a little of
      Cole Porter, after talk about Kierkegaard and
      Kafka should come imitations of Ed Wynn and
      Fields.

          James Thurber

Perseverance is not a long race; it is many short races one after another.

Walter Elliott

The greatest of faults is to be conscious of none.

Thomas Carlyle

Choose in marriage only a woman who you would choose as a friend if she were a man.

Joseph Joubert

One remains young as long as one can still learn, can still take on new habits, can bear contradictions.

Marie von Ebner-Eschenbach

No one is wise enough by himself.

Titus Maccius Plautus (ca. 200 B.C.)

[73]

Truth is such a rare thing, it is delightful to tell it.
Emily Dickinson

To the person with a toothache, even if the world is
tottering, there is nothing more important than
a visit to a dentist.
George Bernard Shaw

Sometimes I think we're alone in the universe, and
sometimes I think we're not. In either case, the
idea is quite staggering.
Arthur C. Clarke

The wise man looks into space, and does not regard
the small as too little, nor the great as too big;
for he knows that there is no limit to
dimensions.

Lao-Tse (6th century B.C.)

There are two kinds of people in the world: those
who come into a room and say, "Here I am!"
and those who come in and say, "Ah, there
you are!"

Anonymous

Humanity takes itself too seriously. It is the world's
original sin. If the cavemen had known how to
laugh, history would have been different.

Oscar Wilde

Borrow trouble for yourself if that's your nature,
but don't lend it to your neighbors.

Rudyard Kipling

If you only keep adding little by little, it will soon
become a big heap.

Hesiod (ca. 700 B.C.)

All the faults of humanity are more pardonable than the means employed to conceal them.

François de La Rochefoucauld
(17th century)

Education should teach us to play the wise fool rather than turn us into the solemn ass.

Kenneth E. Eble

Life appears to me too short to be spent in nursing animosity or registering wrongs.

Charlotte Brontë

Find expression for a sorrow, and it will become dear to you. Find expression for a joy, and you will intensify its ecstasy.

Oscar Wilde

Absolute honesty is as absurd an abstraction as absolute temperature or absolute value.

George Bernard Shaw

[76]

Hope for the best. Expect the worst.
Life is a play. We're unrehearsed.

Mel Brooks

Fools and the wise are equally harmless. It is the half-fools and the half-wise that are dangerous.

Johann Wolfgang von Goethe

Words are, of course, the most powerful drug used by mankind.

Rudyard Kipling

There are two parts to the human dilemma. One is the belief that the end justifies the means. The other is the betrayal of the human spirit.

J. Bronowski

Some pursue happiness—others create it.

Anonymous

Grief can take care of itself, but to get the full value of a joy you must have somebody to divide it with.

Mark Twain

A lifetime of happiness? No man alive could bear it: it would be hell on earth.

George Bernard Shaw

Discovery consists in seeing what everybody has seen and thinking what nobody has thought.

Albert Szent-Györgyi

The only certainty is that nothing is certain.

Pliny, the Elder (1st century A.D.)

All the tools and engines on earth are only extensions of man's limbs and senses.

Ralph Waldo Emerson

Take away memory and your love will no longer exist.

Jessica Julian

The more you listen to the voice within you, the better you will hear what is sounding outside.

Dag Hammarskjöld

Weakness is a greater enemy to virtue than vice.

François de La Rochefoucauld
(17th century)

The only period in life that should give us cause for uncertainty is that brief stretch from the cradle to the grave.

Anonymous

The first problem for all of us, men and women, is not to learn, but to unlearn.

Gloria Steinem

This is the final test of a gentleman: his respect for those who can be of no possible value to him.

William Lyon Phelps

The greatest thing in the world is to know how to be one's own self.

Michel Eyquem de Montaigne
(16 century)

I would rather be the man who bought the Brooklyn Bridge than the man who sold it.

Will Rogers

And walk not on earth exultant. See, you cannot tear open the earth nor can you stretch to the height of the mountains.

Koran (Surah XVII)

The universe begins to look more like a great thought than like a great machine.

Sir James Jeans

Man would indeed be in a poor way if he had to be restrained by fear of punishment and hope of reward after death.

Albert Einstein

An error is more dangerous in proportion to the degree of truth it contains.

Henri Frédéric Amiel

Instead of loving your enemies, treat your friends a little better.

Edgar Watson Howe

In my belief, you cannot deal with the most serious things in the world unless you also understand the most amusing.

Winston Churchill

Things turn out best for people who make the best of the way things turn out.

Anonymous

I expect to pass through life but once. If therefore, there can be any kindness I can show, or any good thing I can do to any fellow being, let me do it now, and not defer or neglect it, as I shall not pass this way again.

William Penn (17th century)

Youth is not a time of life—it is a state of mind.

Anonymous

The cost of a thing is the amount of what I will call life which is required to be exchanged for it, immediately or in the long run.

Henry David Thoreau

The only thing more expensive than education is
    ignorance.
                                    Benjamin Franklin

I look upon the whole world as my fatherland, and
    every war has to me the horror of a family
    feud.
                                    Helen Keller

For me the greatest beauty always lay in the greatest
    clarity.
                            Gotthold Ephraim Lessing

To be alive, to be able to see, to walk, to have
    houses, music, paintings—it's all a miracle. I
    have adopted the technique of living life from
    miracle to miracle.
                                    Artur Rubinstein

Age does not protect you from love. But love, to some extent, protects you from age.

Jeanne Moreau

The eye—it cannot choose but see;
    We cannot bid the ear be still;
    Our bodies feel, where'er they be.
    Against or with our will.

William Wordsworth

I'd rather see folks doubt what's true than accept what isn't.

Frank A. Clark

If dreams all came true, one would fear to fall asleep.

Neil Eskelin

The service we render others is really the rent we pay for our room on earth.

Wilfred Grenfell

[84]

Everything is magic in relations between man and
woman.

Paul Valéry

Horse sense is what keeps horses from betting on
what people will do.

Raymond Nash

We have given so many hostages to fortune.

Lucian (2nd century A.D.)

The duration of our passions no more depends upon
our own will than does the duration of our life.

*François de La Rochefoucauld
(17th century)*

We must believe in free will, we have no choice.

Isaac Bashevis Singer

[85]

What loneliness is more lonely than distrust?
George Eliot

Don't compromise yourself. You are all you've got.
Janis Joplin

As is a tale, so is life; what matters is not how long it is but how good it is.
Lucius Annaeus Seneca
(1st century A.D.)

Ours is a brand-new world of allatonceness. Time has ceased, space has vanished. We now live in a global village.
Marshall McLuhan

When I saw something that needed doing, I did it.
Nellie Cashman

[86]

The great object of life is sensation—to feel that we exist, even in pain.

Lord Byron

Never does a person describe his own character more clearly than by his way of describing that of others.

Jean Paul (Friedrich Richter)

The worst sin towards our fellow-creatures is not to hate them but to be indifferent to them; that's the essence of inhumanity.

George Bernard Shaw

If all that Americans want is security, then they can go to prison. They'll have enough to eat, a bed, and a roof over their heads.

Dwight D. Eisenhower

I'm not convinced that the world is in any worse shape than it ever was. It's just that in this age of almost instantaneous communication, we bear the weight of problems our forefathers only read about after they were solved.

Burton Hillis

The absent are never without fault, nor the present without excuse.

Quoted by Benjamin Franklin

It is better to know nothing than to learn nothing.

Anonymous

You are never fully dressed until you wear a smile.

Charley Willey

I have clearly noticed that often I have one opinion
when I lie down and another one when I stand
up, especially when I have eaten little and
when I am tired.

Georg Christoph Lichtenberg

All is flux, nothing stands still.

Heraclitus (ca. 500 B.C.)

I look to the future, because that's where I'm going to
spend the rest of my life.

George Burns (at age 87)

Without inner peace, it is impossible to have world
peace.

14th Dalai Lama

Nothing in man is more serious than his sense of
humor; it is the sign that he wants all the truth.

Mark Van Doren

Patience and time do more than strength or passion.

Jean de La Fontaine (17th century)

Out yonder there is a huge world, which exists independent of us human beings and which stands before us like a great, eternal riddle, at least partially accessible to our inspection and thinking. The contemplation of this world beckons like a liberation.

Albert Einstein

Wisdom is knowing when you can't be wise.

Paul Engle

Yes: I am a dreamer. For a dreamer is one who can only find his way by moonlight, and his punishment is that he sees the dawn before the rest of the world.

Oscar Wilde

Death means nothing to us: When we are, death has
not come yet, and when death has come, we
no longer are.

Epicurus (ca. 300 B.C.)

My knowledge is like a drop in a vast ocean of
promise.

Tan Sen

It requires a very unusual mind to undertake the
analysis of the obvious.

Alfred North Whitehead

It is not because things are difficult that we do not
dare; it is because we do not dare that they are
difficult.

Lucius Annaeus Seneca
(1st century A.D.)

It is bad manners to say "You are welcome to your own opinion"; but it is the perfection of good fellowship to really mean it.

George Bernard Shaw

I owe all my success in life to having been always a quarter of an hour beforehand.

Horatio Nelson

The person who says it cannot be done should not interrupt the person doing it.

Chinese proverb

Think for yourselves and let others enjoy the right to do the same.

Voltaire

The trouble with most of us is that we would rather be ruined by praise than saved by criticism.

Norman Vincent Peale

Time is like a river of fleeting events, and its current is strong; as soon as something comes into sight, it is swept past us, and something else takes its place, and that too will be swept away.

Marcus Aurelius (2nd century A.D.)

The most important fact about Spaceship Earth: An instruction book didn't come with it.

R. Buckminster Fuller

If you don't like someone, the way he holds his spoon will make you furious; if you do like him, he can turn his plate over into your lap and you won't mind.

Irving Becker

Perfection is finally attained, not when there is no longer anything to add, but when there is no longer anything to take away.

Antoine de Saint-Exupéry

You are what you are when nobody is looking.

Abigail Van Buren ("Dear Abby")
and Ann Landers, twin sisters

Common sense consists in not letting oneself be
dazzled by a sentiment or an idea, however
excellent they may be, to the point of losing
sight of everything else.

André Gide

Imagination was given to man to compensate him for
what he is not, and a sense of humor was
provided to console him for what he is.

Robert Walpole

To be seventy years young is sometimes far more
cheerful and hopeful than to be forty years old.

Oliver Wendell Holmes, Jr.

The essence of courage is not that your heart should not quake, but that nobody else knows that it does.

E. B. Benson

Strengthen yourself with contentment, for it is an impregnable fortress.

Epictetus (1st century A.D.)

Happiness can only be felt if you don't set any condition.

Artur Rubinstein

Search thy own heart; what paineth thee in others in thyself may be.

John Greenleaf Whittier

The best way to make something last is often the belief that it won't.

Gerard de Rohan-Chabot

[95]

The oldest books are still only just out to those who
have not read them.

Samuel Butler (19th century)

Wisdom is to the soul what health is to the body.

François de La Rochefoucauld
(17th century)

After all, the only proper intoxication is
conversation.

Oscar Wilde

You are permitted in time of great danger to walk
with the devil until you have crossed the
bridge.

Bulgarian proverb

Whoever makes the fewest people uneasy is the
best-bred man in the group.

Jonathan Swift

A man is rich in proportion to the things he can afford to let alone.

Henry David Thoreau

The only upright man is he who knows his shortcomings.

Titus Maccius Plautus (ca. 200 B.C.)

You think your pain and your heartbreak are unprecedented in the history of the world, but then you read. It was books that taught me that the things that tormented me most were the very things that connected me with all the people who were alive, or who had ever been alive.

James Baldwin

A maxim is only a clever way of saying something that everyone already knew, but had never quite understood.

Gustav Hasford

Suspect each moment, for it is a thief, tiptoeing away with more than it brings.

John Updike

The same thing happened today that happened yesterday, only to different people.

Walter Winchell

Poor is not the person who has too little, but the person who craves more.

Lucius Annaeus Seneca
(1st century A.D.)

The chief malady of man is a restless curiosity about things that he cannot understand; and it is not so bad for him to be in error as to be curious to no purpose.

Blaise Pascal (17th century)

If you feel that you have both feet planted on level
ground, then the university has failed you.

Robert Goheen

He who goes against the fashion is himself its slave.

Logan Pearsall Smith

Be good enough to remember that your morals are
only your habits; and do not call other people
immoral because they have other habits.

George Bernard Shaw

Cooperation is doing with a smile what you have to
do anyway.

Anonymous

Wise men don't need advice. Fools don't take it.

Benjamin Franklin

Opinion says hot and cold, but the reality is atoms and empty space.

Democritus (ca. 400 B.C.)

A word is not a crystal, transparent and unchanging, it is the skin of a living thought and may vary greatly in color and content according to the circumstances and time in which it is used.

Oliver Wendell Holmes, Jr.

Luck affects everything; let your hook always be cast. In the stream where you least expect it, there will be fish.

Ovid (1st century B.C.)

To educate a man in mind and not in morale is to educate a menace to society.

Theodore Roosevelt

Anyone can be polite to a king, but it takes a
civilized person to be polite to a beggar.
Anonymous

If we could read the secret history of our enemies, we
should find in each man's life sorrow and
suffering enough to disarm all hostility.
Henry Wadsworth Longfellow

The greatest tragedy is indifference.
Red Cross slogan

True politeness is perfect ease and freedom. It simply
consists in treating others just as you love to be
treated yourself.
Earl of Chesterfield

Iron rusts from disuse, stagnant water loses its purity and in cold weather becomes frozen; so does inaction sap the vigors of the mind.

Leonardo da Vinci (ca. 1500)

If you are losing your leisure, look out! You may be losing your soul.

Logan Pearsall Smith

This time, like all times, is a very good one if we but know what to do with it.

Ralph Waldo Emerson

People will cease to commit atrocities only when they cease to believe absurdities.

Voltaire

Liberty is always dangerous, but it is the safest thing we have.

Harry Emerson Fosdick

As long as national sovereignty exists, our only hope is to raise everybody's standard of ethics.

Wernher von Braun

To be truly cultivated is to think reasonably, to live grandly, to love greatly, to shun pettiness, to condemn prejudice and cruelty. In short, to be cultivated is to be alive in the very largest sense.

Dorothy J. Farnan

The test of a man's or woman's breeding is how they behave in a quarrel.

George Bernard Shaw

As a matter of self-preservation, a man needs good friends or ardent enemies, for the former instruct him and the latter take him to task.

Diogenes (4th century B.C.)

[103]

Four be the things I am wiser to know:
 Idleness, sorrow, a friend, and a foe.
Dorothy Parker

There is more to life than increasing its speed.
Mahatma Gandhi

All progress is based upon a universal innate desire
 on the part of every organism to live beyond
 its income.
Samuel Butler (19th century)

A mother is not a person to lean on, but a person to
 make leaning unnecessary.
Dorothy Canfield Fisher

How can they say my life is not a success? Have I
 not for more than 60 years got enough to eat
 and escaped being eaten?
Logan Pearsall Smith

Silence is golden when you can't think of a good
answer.

Anonymous

As we are constituted by nature, there is not a fault
that could not turn into a virtue, not a virtue
that could not turn into a fault.

Johann Wolfgang von Goethe

What we need more than anything else is more
facts about feelings.

Don Robinson

Education is the ability to listen to almost anything
without losing your temper or your self-
confidence.

Robert Frost

He who laughs—lasts.

Wilfred Peterson

There must be no tolerance of intolerance. There must be no freedom to destroy freedom.

Karl Jaspers

Keep your fears to yourself, but share your courage.

Robert Louis Stevenson

For one human being to love another: that is perhaps the most difficult of all tasks, and the ultimate, the last test and proof, the work for which all other work is but preparation.

Rainer Maria Rilke

Never make the mistake of arguing with people for whose opinions you have no respect.

Anonymous

People think responsibility is hard to bear. It's not.
I think that sometimes it is the absence of
responsibility that is harder to bear. You have a
great feeling of impotence.

Henry Kissinger

Certainly it is almost more important how a person
takes his fate than what it is.

Wilhelm von Humboldt

True luck consists not in holding the best cards at the
table: Luckiest he who knows just when to rise
and go home.

John Hay

A good conscience is a continual feast.

Robert Burton

A man should never be ashamed to own he has been in the wrong, which is but saying, in other words, that he is wiser today than he was yesterday.

Alexander Pope

It is not who is right, but what is right, that is important.

Thomas Huxley

The most incomprehensible thing about the world is that it is comprehensible.

Albert Einstein

Character is a by-product; it is produced in the great manufacture of daily duty.

Woodrow Wilson

So they speak soothingly about progress and the greatest possible happiness, forgetting that happiness is itself poisoned if the measure of suffering has not been fulfilled.

Carl Gustav Jung

The value of the average conversation could be enormously improved by the constant use of four simple words: "I do not know."

André Maurois

Anyone who in discussion quotes authority uses his memory rather than his intellect.

Leonardo da Vinci (ca. 1500)

We do not believe in rheumatism and true love until after the first attack.

Marie von Ebner-Eschenbach

To think and to observe humanely means to think and observe apolitically.

Thomas Mann

May you live to be a hundred—and decide the rest for yourself.

Irish proverb

Ours is the age which is proud of machines that think and suspicious of men who try to.

H. M. Jones

Nonviolence is a weapon of the strong.

Mahatma Gandhi

Mishaps are like knives that either serve or cut us as we grasp them by the blade or the handle.

James Russell Lowell

The time is always right to do what is right.

Martin Luther King, Jr.

Explanation given by a pupil for not joining in discussion: "I think I'll learn more by listening. Anything I would say I already know."

Quoted by The Christian Science Monitor

The true mystery of the world is the visible, not the invisible.

Oscar Wilde

Only a weak mind seeks ultimate answers.

Agnes Thornton

The common idea that success spoils people by
making them vain, egotistic, and self-
complacent is erroneous; on the contrary, it
makes them, for the most part, humble,
tolerant, and kind. Failure makes people cruel
and bitter.

William Somerset Maugham

Act only on that principle whereby you can at the
same time want that it should become a
universal law.

Immanuel Kant

Choose always the way that seems the best,
however rough it may be; custom will soon
render it easy and agreeable.

Pythagoras (6th century B.C.)

Knowledge is not a loose-leaf notebook of facts.
Above all, it is a responsibility for the integrity
of what we are, primarily of what we are as
ethical creatures.

J. Bronowski

The chains of habit are too weak to be felt until they
are too strong to be broken.

Samuel Johnson

The surest cure for vanity is loneliness.

Thomas Wolfe

Human felicity is produced not so much by great
pieces of good fortune that seldom happen, as
by little advantages that occur every day.

Benjamin Franklin

Laughter has no foreign accent.

Paul B. Lowney

[113]

For most men life is a search for the proper manila
    envelope in which to get themselves filed.
                    Clifton Fadiman

The universe is change; our life is what our thoughts
    make of it.

                    Marcus Aurelius (2nd century A.D.)

There is one thing which gives radiance to
    everything. It is the idea of something around
    the corner.
                    G. K. Chesterton

Life does not cease to be funny when people die, any
    more than it ceases to be serious when people
    laugh.
                    George Bernard Shaw

Happiness is often the result of being too busy to be miserable.

Anonymous

Always be a littler kinder than necessary.

James M. Barrie

Nine-tenths of wisdom is being wise in time.

Theodore Roosevelt

The absence of alternatives clears the mind marvelously.

Henry Kissinger

Our country, right or wrong! When right, to be kept right; when wrong, to be put right.

Carl Schurz
(1872, addressing Congress)

At the beginning of a marriage ask yourself whether this woman will be interesting to *talk* to from now until old age.

Friedrich Nietzsche

In everything one must consider the end.

Jean de La Fontaine (17th century)

Such is the state of life that none are happy but by the anticipation of change. The change itself is nothing. When we have made it, the next wish is to change again.

Samuel Johnson

More important than learning how to recall things is finding ways to forget things that are cluttering the mind.

Eric Butterworth

[116]

Nature goes her way, and all that to us seems an exception is really according to order.

Johann Wolfgang von Goethe

Dost thou love life? Then do not squander time; for that's the stuff life is made of.

Quoted by Benjamin Franklin

The trouble with the world is that the stupid are cocksure and the intelligent are full of doubt.

Bertrand Russell

More important than the quest for certainty is the quest for clarity.

François Gautier

A man's reach should exceed his grasp,
Or what's a heaven for?

Robert Browning

[117]

People change and forget to tell each other.
Lillian Hellman

The superfluous, a very necessary thing.
Voltaire

Only a mediocre person is always at his best.
William Somerset Maugham

There's only one success—to be able to spend your life in your own way.
Christopher Morley

Commonplace love: Often it is the only kind possible. . . . To help others as best you can, to avoid losing your temper, to be understanding, to keep calm and smiling (as much as possible!) is loving your neighbor, without fancy talk, but in a practical way.
Pope John Paul I

While we have prisons, it matters little which of us occupy the cells.

George Bernard Shaw

Much unhappiness results from our inability to remember the nice things that happen to us.

W. N. Rieger

No man can prove upon awakening that he is the man who he thinks went to bed the night before, or that anything that he recollects is anything other than a convincing dream.

R. Buckminster Fuller

Everyone complains about his memory, and no one complains about his judgment.

François de La Rochefoucauld (17th century)

Love doesn't just sit there, like a stone; it has to be made, like bread; remade all the time, made new.

Ursula K. Le Guin

There is a rule in sailing where the more maneuverable ship should give way to the less maneuverable craft. I think this is sometimes a good rule to follow in human relationships as well.

Joyce Brothers

Those who plow the sea do not carry the winds in their hands.

Publilius Syrus (ca. 50 B.C.)

Every extension of knowledge arises from making the conscious the unconscious.

Friedrich Nietzsche

H ave nothing in your house that you do not know
to be useful, or believe to be beautiful.
William Morris

R eading makes a full man, conference a ready man,
and writing an exact man.
Francis Bacon (ca. 1600)

L ove does not consist in gazing at each other but in
looking outward in the same direction.
Antoine de Saint-Exupéry

W hat do we live for if it is not to make life less
difficult for each other?
George Eliot

S ome people speak from experience, while others,
from experience, don't speak.
Anonymous

[121]

A life spent in making mistakes is not only more honorable but more useful than a life spent in doing nothing.

George Bernard Shaw

W hen the universe has crushed him, the human being will still be nobler than that which kills him, because he knows that he is dying, and of its victory the universe knows nothing.

Blaise Pascal (17th century)

T ruth is the kind of error without which a certain species of life could not live. What ultimately counts is the value for *life*.

Friedrich Nietzsche

T he greatest good you can do for another is not just to share your riches but to reveal to him his own.

Benjamin Disraeli

[122]

Always do right. This will gratify some people, and astonish the rest.

Mark Twain

Any man more right than his neighbors constitutes a majority of one.

Henry David Thoreau

We must select the illusion which appeals to our temperament, and embrace it with passion if we want to be happy.

Cyril Connolly

Fill the unforgiving minute with sixty seconds' worth of distance run.

Rudyard Kipling

The wrongdoer is often the person who has left something undone rather than the person who has done something.

Marcus Aurelius (2nd century A.D.)

Genius is one percent inspiration and ninety-nine percent perspiration.

Thomas Alva Edison

Humor is an affirmation of dignity, a declaration of our superiority to all that befalls us.

Romain Gary

Life is painting a picture, not doing a sum.

Oliver Wendell Holmes, Jr.

The willingness to trust others even when you know you may be taken advantage of is the cornerstone of becoming civilized.

O. A. Battista

Seize from every moment its unique novelty, and do not prepare your joys.

André Gide

Have patience with all things, but first of all with yourself.

St. Francis of Sales (ca. 1600)

The world is one percent good, one percent bad, ninety-eight percent neutral. It can go one way or the other, depending on which side is pushing. This is why what individuals do is important.

Hans Habe

If you can put the question "Am I or am I not responsible for my acts?" then you are responsible.

Feodor Dostoevsky

When you're through learning, you're through.
Vernon Law

We don't remain good if we don't always strive to
become better.
Gottfried Keller

The clearest sign of wisdom is continued cheerfulness.
Michel Eyquem de Montaigne
(16th century)

Today is the first day of the rest of your life.
Abbie Hoffman

The world belongs to the enthusiast who keeps cool.
William McFee

I would like to render—all through my life, at the
   slightest touch—a sound that is pure, clean,
   authentic. Nearly every human note I have
   heard sounds wrong.
                                          André Gide

Success comes before work only in the dictionary.
                                          Anonymous

The most important words we'll ever utter are those
   words we say to ourselves, about ourselves,
   when we're by ourselves.
                                          Al Walker

Three passions, simple but overwhelmingly strong,
   have governed my life: the longing for love,
   the search for knowledge, and unbearable pity
   for the suffering of mankind.
                                          Bertrand Russell

A thing of beauty is a joy forever:
   Its loveliness increases; it will never
   Pass into nothingness; but still will keep
   A bower quiet for us, and a sleep
   Full of sweet dreams, and health,
      and quiet breathing.

John Keats

I don't pretend we have the answers. But the
   questions are certainly worth thinking about.

Arthur C. Clarke

The most exhausting thing in life, I have discovered,
   is being insincere.

Anne Morrow Lindbergh

One disadvantage of having nothing to do is you
   can't stop and rest.

Franklin P. Jones

[128]

In this era of world wars, in this atomic age, values have changed. We have learned that we are the guests of existence, travelers between two stations. We must discover security within ourselves.

Boris Pasternak

I honestly think it is better to be a failure at something you love than to be a success at something you hate.

George Burns

If liberty means anything at all, it means the right to tell people what they do not want to hear.

George Orwell

If you can spend a perfectly useless afternoon in a perfectly useless manner, you have learned how to live.

Lin Yutang

As a rule, I always look for what others ignore.
Marshall McLuhan

See how fleeting and trifling is the condition of
humans; yesterday an embryo, tomorrow a
mummy or ashes. So for the tiny sliver of time
that you are given, live rationally, and depart
from life cheerfully, the way the ripe olive
falls, praising the season that brought it forth
and the tree that nurtured it.
Marcus Aurelius (2nd century A.D.)

It isn't the mountains ahead that wear you out. It's the
grain of sand in your shoe.
Anonymous

The greatest use of a life is to spend it on something
that will outlast it.
William James

[130]

Is not life a hundred times too short for us to bore
ourselves?

Friedrich Nietzsche

The nicest thing about the future is that it comes one
day at a time.

Anonymous

To be without some of the things you want is an
indispensable part of happiness.

Bertrand Russell

The sound of laughter has always seemed to me the
most civilized music in the universe.

Peter Ustinov

I think the years I have spent in prison have been the
   most formative and important in my life
   because of the discipline, the sensations, but
   chiefly the opportunity to think clearly, to try
   to understand things.
                    Jawaharlal Nehru

To cheat oneself out of love is the most terrible
   deception; it is an eternal loss for which there is
   no reparation, either in time or in eternity.
                    Sören Kierkegaard

Affection is the broadest basis of good in life.
                    George Eliot

A man's rootage is more important than his leafage.
                    Woodrow Wilson

If people are taught how to think and not always what to think, a false concept will be guarded against.

Georg Christoph Lichtenberg

There is no one else who can ever fill your role in the same way, so it's a good idea to perform it as well as possible.

Humphry Osmond

There is nothing in the world more pitiable than the man who goes about telling his friends that life is not worth living, when they know perfectly well that if he meant it he could stop living much more easily than go on eating.

George Bernard Shaw

The test of good manners is to be able to put up pleasantly with bad ones.

Anonymous

[133]

The most beautiful thing we can experience is the mysterious. It is the source of all true art and science.

Albert Einstein

If you are able to say how much you love, you love little.

Petrarch (ca. 1350)

Experience is a good school, but the fees are high.

Heinrich Heine

Better ask twice than lose your way once.

Danish proverb

It is not true that we have only one life to live; if we can read, we can live as many lives and as many kinds of lives as we wish.

S. I. Hayakawa

No man is good enough to govern another man
without that other man's consent.

Abraham Lincoln

"People's minds are trained largely at the expense
of their hearts." This is not so; it is only that
there are more educable minds than there are
educable hearts.

Marie von Ebner-Eschenbach

And we ask not any soul to perform beyond its
scope.

Koran (Surah XXIII)

Philosophy triumphs easily over past evils and future
evils. But present evils triumph over it.

François de La Rochefoucauld
(17th century)

Moral certainty is always a sign of cultural inferiority. The more uncivilized the man, the surer he is that he knows precisely what is right and what is wrong.

H. L. Mencken

Everything leads us to believe that there exists a certain point of the intelligence at which life and death, the real and the imaginary, the past and the future . . . cease to be perceived as opposites.

André Breton

Be happy. It is a way of being wise.

Colette

The simplest things give me ideas.

Joan Miró

If we're told that an odd piece of our china is worth a hundred pounds, —how rare its beauty!

Logan Pearsall Smith

Marriages are made in heaven and consummated on earth.

French saying

Advice is what we ask for when we already know the answer but wish we didn't.

Erica Jong

Quality is a proud and soaring thing.

Jessica Julian

I like the dreams of the future better than the history of the past.

Thomas Jefferson

The longest day is soon ended.

Pliny, the Younger (ca. 100 A.D.)

Who, being loved, is poor?

Oscar Wilde

Reality is nothing but a collective hunch.

Lily Tomlin

It often takes more courage to change one's opinion
than to stick to it.

Georg Christoph Lichtenberg

Never put off until tomorrow what you can do
today, because if you enjoy it today, you can
do it again tomorrow.

Anonymous

One should, every day at least, hear a little song, read a good poem, see a fine picture, and, if possible, speak a few reasonable words.

Johann Wolfgang von Goethe

It's very hard to take yourself too seriously when you look at the world from outer space.

Thomas K. Mattingly II
(Apollo 16 astronaut)

Nature, to be commanded, must be obeyed.

Francis Bacon (ca. 1600)

Fraudulent is the person who persuades himself that he is *justified* in doing the things he feels like doing—who places his reasoning at the service of his desires, of his self-interest (which is worse), or of his nature.

André Gide

[139]

People who fight fire with fire usually end up with ashes.

Abigail Van Buren ("Dear Abby")

Do not count your chickens before they are hatched.

Aesop (ca. 550 B.C.)

I like trees because they seem more resigned to the way they have to live than other things do.

Willa Cather

I am a human being: nothing human is alien to me.

Terence (2nd century B.C.)

Only a life in the service of others is worth living.

Albert Einstein

We are all happy if we only knew it.

Feodor Dostoevsky

A wise man will desire no more than what he may get justly, use soberly, distribute cheerfully, and leave contently.

Quoted by Benjamin Franklin

What lies behind us and what lies before us are tiny matters compared with what lies within us.

Anonymous

The sun is new each day.

Heraclitus (ca. 500 B.C.)

Every person bears the whole stamp of the human condition.

*Michel Eyquem de Montaigne
(16th century)*

[141]

Few blame themselves until they have exhausted all
other possibilities.
Anonymous

The most important thing that parents can teach their
children is how to get along without them.
Frank A. Clark

The only person who behaves sensibly is my tailor.
He takes my measure anew every time he sees
me. All the rest go on with their old
measurements.
George Bernard Shaw

Hear the other side.
Roman law principle

[142]

Millions long for immortality who do not know
what to do with themselves on a rainy Sunday
afternoon.

Susan Ertz

I always say to myself, what is the most important
thing we can think about at this extraordinary
moment.

R. Buckminster Fuller

If you would be pungent, be brief; for it is with
words as with sunbeams. The more they are
condensed, the deeper they burn.

Robert Southey

Three things in human life are important: The first is
to be kind. The second is to be kind. And the
third is to be kind.

Henry James

The difference between the right word and the almost
right word is the difference between lightning
and the lightning bug.
Mark Twain

It ain't over till it's over.
Lawrence ("Yogi") Berra

He was a bold man that first ate an oyster.
Jonathan Swift

The final mystery is oneself.
Oscar Wilde

Index of Sources

[146]

[149]

About the Authors

Jerome Agel's more than forty major books include collaborations with Marshall McLuhan, Carl Sagan, Stanley Kubrick, Herman Kahn, and Isaac Asimov. His most recent works include the nonfiction novel *Deliverance in Shanghai* and *The U.S. Constitution for Everyone*.

Walter D. Glanze is the author or editor of fifty-two reference works and the editor of over two hundred books on a large variety of subjects. Among his most recent works is *The Language of Sex from A to Z*.